ideals EASTER

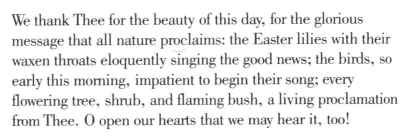

We thank Thee for the beauty of this day, for the glorious message that all nature proclaims: the Easter lilies with their waxen throats eloquently singing the good news; the birds, so early this morning, impatient to begin their song; every flowering tree, shrub, and flaming bush, a living proclamation from Thee. O open our hearts that we may hear it, too!

In Thy presence restore our faith, our hope, our joy. Grant to our spirits refreshment, rest, and peace. Maintain within our hearts an unruffled calm, an unbroken serenity that no storms of life shall ever be able to take from us.

Peter Marshall

ISBN 0-8249-1060-5

Publisher, Patricia A. Pingry
Editor, Peggy Schaefer
Art Director, Patrick McRae
Production Manager, Jan Johnson
Editorial Assistant, Kathleen Gilbert
Copy Editor, Joan Anderson

IDEALS/vol. 45, No. 2 March MCMLXXXVIII IDEALS (ISSN 0019-137X) is published eight times a year, February, March, May, June, August, September, November, December
by IDEALS PUBLISHING CORPORATION, Nelson Place at Elm Hill Pike, Nashville, Tenn. 37214
Second class postage paid at Nashville, Tennessee, and additional mailing offices.
Copyright © MCMLXXXVIII by IDEALS PUBLISHING CORPORATION
POSTMASTER: Send address changes to Ideals, Post Office Box 148000, Nashville, Tenn. 37214-8000
All rights reserved. Title IDEALS registered U.S. Patent Office.

SINGLE ISSUE—$3.95
ONE-YEAR SUBSCRIPTION—eight consecutive issues as published—$17.95
TWO-YEAR SUBSCRIPTION—sixteen consecutive issues as published—$31.95
Outside U.S.A., add $4.00 per subscription year for postage and handling.

Front and back covers from Grant Heilman Photography

Inside front cover by Fred Sieb
Inside back cover from FPG International

Last Snow

Lolita Pinney

A blanket of snow fell, belated and chill.
My case of spring fever is arrested and still.

The last wintry blast blows its way through the land,
Defying the forecasts of spring here at hand.

Don't bring out the yard tools! No fertilizer, please!
Forget about crocuses and leafy, young trees . . .

But just as my footsteps drag over the hill,
A small, stubborn robin lifts his voice in a trill.

And suddenly gloom fades, and my spirits sing:
"It's JUST the LAST SNOW! Very soon 'twill be spring."

Photo Opposite
SPRING SNOW
Gay Bumgarner

Song of the Woods

LaVerne P. Larson

The lace-edged dawn with rosy glow
Weaves ropes of golden light,
As darkness spreads its velvet wings
And silently takes flight.

Woodland trails begin to sing
Sweet magic melodies,
As nature stirs and slowly wakes
With soft and gentle breeze.

The brown earth, rich and warm again,
Grows green with promise fair;
A sweet perfume of earth and wood
Floats on the balmy air.

Each woodland creature, bright-eyed now
From quiet winter rest,
Begins to scamper to and fro,
Quite filled with glee and zest.

The sun's rays kiss the woodland trails
As does the silver rain;
And when a rainbow bridge appears,
The world is bright again.

Beauty, peace, and happiness
Dwell o'er the woodland sod,
For all the trails are tended
By the gentle hands of God.

Photo Opposite
REDWOOD NATIONAL PARK
Monserrate Schwartz

It's April

Edith M. Helstern

When the skies are blue as heather
And the days are lingering late,
With a soft breeze in the weather,
It's April—at our gate.

When the buds lift up their faces
To the touch of warm spring rain,
And tulips bloom in numbers,
It's April—once again.

When the earth awakes with sleepy eyes,
As soft rain taps her door,
And bids her flowered family rise,
Then spring is here—once more.

It comes all dressed in colors
And blossoms in array,
And never is more beautiful
Than spring—on Easter Day.

Photo Opposite
TULIP DELIGHT
Fred M. Dole Productions

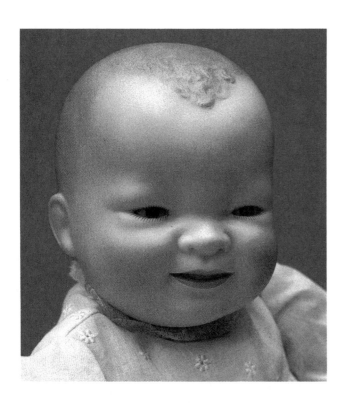

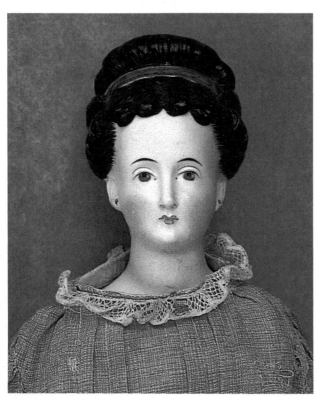

From the sophisticated royalty of Europe to babies learning to crawl, millions of people adore dolls. Today, collecting dolls is recognized as a major adult hobby with devoted followers. After all, a doll can evoke a memory of a hand-crafted gift from a loving grandmother, or be a harbinger of fashion wearing the latest designs of Paris.

There are numerous modern dolls, but it is the older creations of the nineteenth century, the golden age of doll making, which cast the strongest spell on collectors. Usually dolls are identified by the material from which the heads are formed. China, parian, and bisque dolls all started out as liquid forms of clay slip. Doll makers poured the liquid into molds and then fired the clay form in huge factory kilns. They then sanded and decorated the heads. The way they finished each head determined how it was classified.

China, the oldest category, is easy to recognize. The glazed texture of a china has the same shiny surface as plates used for eating. The style of the molded hair determines the collectibility. Dolls with short black painted waves low on the forehead are the most common. Chinas were made from the middle 1700s to the 1930s, when war disrupted doll making in Germany.

In contrast to the more humble chinas, the parians are elegant ladies with molded hair. The elaborate coiffures are often decorated with clay ribbons, ruffles, and flowers applied by hand. The decorations make a striking contrast to the faces, reminding one of a tantalizing birthday cake. Parians usually have light brown or dark blond hair, and the best were produced in the 1870s, mostly in Germany.

Each material has its own fans, but currently the collector's market most highly values bisque heads. A head is classified as bisque if the complexion is tinted a flesh tone and left unglazed. From the 1850s through the 1930s, Germany, France, and Japan produced haughty ladies, laughing children, and chubby babies of bisque. Bisque girl dolls from the early 1900s and 1930s have open mouths with teeth, sleeping glass eyes, and bland expressions. Closed-mouth specimens and characters with exaggerated features are more prized because fewer were produced.

For years the ultimate in collecting has been French bisque

dolls. Costumed in intricate fashions, their haunting faces and paperweight eyes can warm the heart of even the most objective viewer. To create the lifelike eyes, doll makers added a crystal dome over the multicolored blown glass iris. After being fired in a kiln to fuse the two parts, the eyes have the amazing appearance of luminous depth, just as a human eye does.

In the nineteenth century, French factories such as Jumeau assigned workers a specific feature to decorate. The practice of painting the same features day after day created a mastery of decorating which has never been equaled. The complexion of the doll can be as delicate as a young lady's blush. The multi-stroke eyebrows of antique dolls display an artist's touch that even the modern airgun can't duplicate.

Knowing the manufacturer of a doll is vital to today's serious collector. Fortunately, many companies incised mold numbers, initials, and names on the back of the heads. For example, a head with the name "Hilda" was made by the German firm Kestner. If the word "Bru" is on the doll, it is a valuable French creation. Besides the marks on dolls, collectors also search for examples which started a trend or evoke a pleasant childhood memory. The Bye-lo, copyrighted by Grace Storey Putnam in 1922, represented a three-day-old infant and a break with the tradition that baby dolls should appear to be at least a year old. Every grandmother, mother, and aunt was reminded of a newborn baby. And the charm still works.

The Kewpie dolls designed by Rose O'Neill are also favorites. These little imps with their blue wings and red paper hearts on the stomachs are messengers of love. In the 1920s, Kewpies dressed as brides and grooms in crepe paper decorated many wedding cakes. Kewpie dolls are still in production, but the old bisque examples are the most popular with collectors.

Some collectors desire dolls with a documented past because they are three-dimensional lessons in history. Others prefer dolls that are pretty, and some like those that are homely. But whatever the reason, if the doll brings pleasure, it has achieved its purpose.

Judith Whorton

Photos from the collection of Judith Whorton

Migrant Beauty

Cora Ellen Wells

I wonder where the bluebirds dip their coats
And if the pigment, fresh as morning dew,
Is brought from fairy lands in magic boats
Across the skyward seas to catch the blue.
I wonder if their songs so sweet and true
Are captured from the skies where silver floats
Go sailing by, while beauty drifts anew
Into my heart each time I hear their notes.

I love the days when bluebirds dot the plain
And often come to preen beside my door,
When spring has caught the bright and golden strain
Of music tossed from heaven's topaz shore,
When earth awakes and chords of love's refrain
Are sent from God on migrant wings once more.

Photo Opposite
NESTING BLUEBIRD
Heather Davidson

Photo Overleaf
SPRING GARDEN
Larry Lefever
Grant Heilman Photography

Song of Easter

J. Harold Gwynne, D.D.

Easter is a happy time—
Gay festival of spring—
When human hearts are lifted up,
And nature's voices sing.

Easter is a sacred time
Because Christ rose again,
And brought new hope to all the world,
And gave new life to men.

Easter is a lovely time
Of joy and healing light,
Of music that inspires the soul,
Of lilies gleaming white.

Easter is a giving time
For fellowship with friends,
A time for sweet remembering
Of love that never ends.

Easter is a hopeful time
Filled with faith and love,
And thoughts of life reserved for us
In paradise above.

Bible Book Cover

Ann Marie Braaten

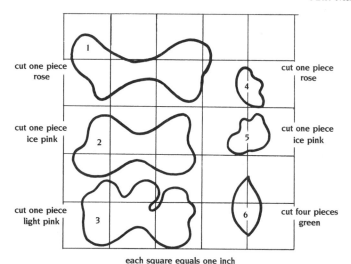

each square equals one inch

Materials Needed:

(Makes one cover for a bible 5¾ inches wide by 8 inches high by 1¼ inches thick. You may need to increase the amount of yard goods for larger bible covers.)
⅜ **yard white broadcloth**
⅜ **yard needle punch fabric**
1¼ **yard pre-gathered white lace, ½-inch wide**
⅛ **yard fusible interfacing**
¾ **yard satin ribbon, ⅜-inch wide**
Pink and green broadcloth scraps
Matching thread

Book Cover Pattern:

Using the following formula, cut a rectangular pattern out of paper for the book cover.

Measure the length: 2 times width of book plus thickness of book plus 1 inch (for seams) plus ½ inch (for ease).

Measure the width: height of book plus 1 inch (for seams) plus ½ inch (for ease).

Construction:

Step One: Cutting Book Cover Pieces

Pin pattern to white broadcloth. Cut two pieces.

Pin pattern to needle punch fabric. Cut one piece.

Measure and cut two additional pieces from white broadcloth using the width of book cover pattern by 4 inches. These will be the pocket ends.

Step Two: Preparing the Appliqué

Press interfacing onto pink and green broadcloth pieces.

Pin appliqué pattern pieces to colored fabric (see diagram above) and cut shapes.

Step Three: Attaching the Lace Edging

With right sides together, pin lace to one of the broadcloth pieces which has been placed on the needle punch fabric. Machine baste along the edge of the lace, leaving a ½-inch seam allowance along broadcloth edges.

Step Four: Attaching the Appliqués

Pin and sew each shape, one at a time, to book cover front (the form to which lace has been basted), changing thread to match the color of each shape. (A fine stitch length with a medium zigzag works best.)

Begin with shape 1 and continue pinning and sewing through shape 6, using the photograph as a positioning and color guide.

Step Five: Preparing Pocket Ends

Prepare each end by pressing under one long side ¼ inch. Press under ¼ inch again. Sew along fold to finish edge.

With right sides together, baste pocket pieces to each end of book cover front.

Step Six: Finishing the Book Cover

Cut the satin ribbon in half. With right sides of ribbons down on book cover front, baste them to center of top seam.

With right sides together, pin cover back to front. Sew along outer edges, using a ½-inch seam allowance. (Make sure loose ribbon ends are free of seam line.) Leave a 2½-inch edge at top left corner for turning.

Clip corners. Pull book cover through opening.

Press lightly. Slip-stitch opening closed.

Photo Opposite
BIBLE COVER
Nancy Robinson

Restless

Dorothy Bettencourt Elfstrom

Like a sea gull I ever am restless
As I travel the voyage of life;
My dreams are the wings that transport me
Away from the cares and the strife

Of the routinous things that grow boresome.
My soul craves adventure—romance!
I thrill to the sound of great music;
My feet long to march and to dance.

Sometimes when the world bears down
Like a cage with iron bars,
I gaze at the blue sky above me
And find freedom among the stars,

Or in the sweet song of the robin,
Or the waves of the onrushing sea;
Somehow I feel kin to the ocean,
It, too, seems restless like me.

My heart seeks the hearts of others,
My mind, greater knowledge of things;
And I'm thankful that I was born restless
With the thundering urge of wings.

Rendezvous

Grace E. Easley

I cannot do my work today,
A butterfly is on the fence,
And though I try to concentrate,
I've given up the dull pretense.
How can I think of anything,
When skies are blue and clouds are white,
And crystal waters ripple so,
And little forest trails invite?

I have a rendezvous to keep,
With long-awaited spring this year.
Oh, do not scold me if I seem,
A little absent-minded, dear!
There is a sunny, windblown hill,
Just waiting there for me to climb.
Pack up a lunch and come with me,
There'll never be a better time!

Look how the ivy hugs the wall,
See how the squirrels run and play!
I am a miser who cannot
Afford to waste a single day!
Oh can't you feel it everywhere?
Impossible it's only me,
Caught up within the age-old charm,
Of springtime's flowered sorcery!

It's Always Easter

Patricia Ann Emme

It's always Easter in the hearts
Of those who share Christ's love.
Upon his face the light of grace
Shines down from up above.

It's always Easter in the hearts
Of those who walk his way.
The cross of Calvary shines bright
And lights a path each day.

It's always Easter in the hearts
Of those who look and see
The resurrected King of Kings
Who lives for you and me.

Children in the Sun

Sondra Pohlmann Harrold

Run, run, my little ones,
Under the golden sun.

Let your spirits like eagles soar,
Let your laughter like lions roar,

Sing a song so joyous and strong,
Borne on the wind the whole day long.

Dance and play on this glad day;
Here no troubles will come your way.

Like the sunrise we'll pretend
That this day will never end.

Dreams we'll share together here,
Later pursue them without fear.

Run, run, my little ones,
Under God's golden sun.

April Recipe

Catherine Grayman

Mix tulips, crocuses, daffodils,
And puffs of brisk clean air
With violets in the greening grass
And new buds everywhere;

Take wayward kites, the songs of birds,
White fluffy clouds or rain,
Wrap in a month of ecstacy
And serve April days again.

Reflections

April Day

Rita Farnham

Through emerald leaves
The violet peeps,
Her shy head bending low,
While daffodils
In yellow hats
Are nodding to and fro.
The buttercups,
And tulips, too,
Are whispering
In the breeze
At tiny furry catkins
On pussy willow trees.

It's spring! It's spring!
The bluebird's song
Begins at break of dawn,
And sunbeams dance
From drops of dew
That sparkle on the lawn.
The dogwood on the hillside,
The redbud blossoms gay,
And lilacs by the doorside
Proclaim this April day.

One Daffodil

Carol Ann Kimball

One tiny, golden daffodil
Emerged in early spring.
It gave me joy, this sunshine-cradled,
Beautiful, growing thing.

Then my son was at the door,
Boyish, shy, half-still.
His small, fat hand in wonder held
My one bright daffodil.

"For you," he grinned, and he was proud,
While I, in disarray,
Heard SLAM! (the door) as he ran out
To wander through the day.

Next week I'll have a dozen 'dils
That we can all enjoy,
But for today, and always, I'll have
Just one little boy.

Editor's Note: Readers are invited to submit unpublished, original poetry, short anecdotes, and humorous reflections on life for possible publication in future I*deals* issues. Please send copies only; manuscripts will not be returned. Writers will receive $10 for each published submission. Send materials to "Readers' Reflections," Ideals Publishing Corporation, Nelson Place at Elm Hill Pike, Nashville, Tennessee 37214.

Recipe for Spring

Clare Curley

If I could fill a crystal glass
With sparkling, gold sunshine
And add a little patch of sky,
Azure and hyaline;

If I could sprinkle dewdrops in
A little gypsy breeze,
A dozen fairy's handkerchiefs
The color of the leaves;

And then if I could mix them up
And take a look inside,
I'd see a lovely springtime scene
Down by the countryside.

There'd be a meadow, showing signs
Of springtime's golden glow,
And where the last of winter lay—
Daffodils in the snow!

Renewal of the Soul

Gertrude Rudberg

Easter is to everyone
Renewal of the soul
When spring bursts forth with songs of birds
After winter cold.

It fills our hearts with hopefulness,
Its promise is sublime
Of life renewed and souls restored
In every earthly clime.

It lights the way in caverns dark
Where fear we've felt and seen,
And melts the frozen rivulets
Of doubting in between.

It paints the heavens bright with blue,
Embroiders them with lace,
Where we recall our risen Lord
Ascended there in grace.

The Little Town Church

Loise Pinkerton Fritz

Springtime has come to the little town church,
The little town church of white.
The spreading, lone forsythia
Is covered with florets bright.
Beautiful florets of yellowish-gold
That brighten the still-dull earth;
Springtime has come in a colorful dress,
And come to this small-town church.

Easter has come to the little town church,
The little town church I know.
The choir is singing, "Christ's risen today,"
While bells chime sounds of hope.
Easter has come to the little town church,
To churches in cities and dells.
And the Christ of Easter shall come and dwell
In the hearts of the people, as well.

Small Green Thumb

Leone Monroe

She plants her seeds as I plant mine;
We water them together.
And in her eyes bright visions shine
Of blooms in sunny weather.

Although my rows don't yield a thing
But weeds and straggly flowers,
I know the gracious hand of spring
Most surely will endow hers

With matchless blossoms, each a prize,
For no one yet has told her
That beauty lies within the eyes
(And age) of the beholder.

April in My Own Backyard

Edna Jaques

April in my own backyard:
Lettuce, peppergrass, and chard
Send up tender baby leaves,
While a mother robin weaves
Such a wee fantastic bed
In the branches overhead.

There against the crannied wall,
Clothed in lichen like a shawl,
Little niches fill with moss
(An old clothesline is thrown across),
And there a toadstool white and round,
Like a teepee, stands its ground.

In the corners cobwebs cling,
Mystic emblems of the spring,
Hued like opals in the sun;
Gay petunias one by one,
Colorful as patchwork quilts,
Blow and part like Highland kilts.

Ash and thorn and stunted pine,
Peeping o'er the fence of mine,
Little wildlings yet a part
Of the spring's great pulsing heart,
Lawns all green and daisy starred—
These are April in my yard.

Relics of an Old-World Easter

Walter J. Wentz

As winter snows receded and the sun rose higher each day to herald the coming spring, peasant women of the Ukraine prepared to celebrate the Resurrection with an art form older than Christianity.

Their symbols of spring's rebirth and fertility were tiny, vivid masterpieces—geometric patterns of flowers, animals, intricate cross-hatchings, and complex borders, all full of ancient meaning and glowing with the colors of natural dyes.

And the "canvas" upon which the peasant women worked was the most fragile and delicate imaginable—a new-laid hen's egg.

Ukrainian Easter eggs, once limited to the steppes and forests of southwestern Russia and produced in patterns handed down from mother to daughter for centuries, are today recognized as treasures of folk art. Private collections and museums cherish outstanding examples of *pysanky*—"written eggs"— some specimens being fifty or eighty years old. And the creation of pysanky has spread far beyond the Ukraine, as emigrants and their descendants, and modern craftspeople as well, have revived the ancient art.

Technically, the creation of Ukrainian Easter eggs is fairly simple, rather like batik, in which lines of melted beeswax shield parts of a design from repeated dye-baths. But spiritually and esthetically, far more is involved.

Long ago, the egg itself was deeply significant. To the pagans of old it symbolized the primeval world-egg, from which all creation was hatched. Broken open, it revealed the yellow yolk, like the brilliant sun-god who was reborn each spring to rescue the world from the dark grip of winter. And, like the quickening earth, the egg could mysteriously bring forth new life. Small wonder that it was venerated and became the basis for a sacred art, replete with powerful symbols.

After Christianity came to the Ukraine, those ancient symbols were converted to Christian meanings—and the creation of pysanky continued, with the blessing of the church, as a ritual of Easter.

While modern collectors and craftspeople enjoy the beauty of these eggs, in the Ukraine, and in traditional Ukrainian households in America,
pysanky have served many purposes.

Different blessings were invoked upon every egg. Some psanky were intended as gifts between friends and relatives. A bowl of pysanky in the home was said to keep fire and lightning away and bring good luck and happiness.

Pysanky were tokens of love when given by a girl to a boy. A young bride was presented with a pysanka decorated with the image of a hen, ancient symbol of fertility; if no children were forthcoming, her husband was then presented a pysanka decorated with a rooster. Children were given eggs decorated with flowers and incorporating large areas of the white of innocence; old people were given pysanky in darker colors, decorated with the gates and ladders which symbolize the transition to another world.

The farmer buried special pysanky in his fields, or fed his farm animals decorated eggs to increase their fertility; eggs were hung in barns to protect them, and buried beneath the foundations of a new house. Everywhere, pysanky were designed to repel evil and strengthen goodness. Symbols, colors, prayers, and blessings by the village priest all gave added power to the Easter eggs.

Every spring, the old Ukrainians said, the Evil One traveled the world to see how many pysanky had been made that year. If few were to be found, he was encouraged to extend his dark dominion; if many were visible, he withdrew in fear. The ancient spiral pattern, dating far back into prehistory, was a particularly effective trap for wandering demons. Attracted to the inward-turning design, they were imprisoned forever at its center.

The most powerful and sacred of the old symbols was, of course, the sun—originally representing the sun-god, later Christ. Birds represented spring, rebirth, good fortune. Stags or goats invoked wealth. Triangles stood for the Trinity. Circles and meanders represented supernatural protection and everlasting life. All these, with many others, are still incorporated into the tiny, brilliant works of art created by the women of the Ukraine—to be given and treasured as symbols of the annual miracle of rebirth, and of the strong bonds between the Ukrainian people and their ancient heritage.

Photo Opposite
RUSSIAN EGGS
Gerald Koser

Voice of Youth

Dan A. Hoover

How beautiful it is to hear
The voices of the young,
And let our hearts be lifted by
The melody they have sung.

The dawn of spring is filled with song
Of birds, and breeze, and rain.
Have you not been quickened
By their lilting springtime strains?

But in this complex world of ours,
There is not anything
As stirring as the voice of youth
Who worship Him and sing.

Easter Bells

Joy Belle Burgess

The beauty of the Easter bells—
Ethereal and real—
Thrills the waking earth with sounds
Of clear, ringing peals.

And joy comes with the dawning light
When bells are in their prime.
Ebullient sound of hope and love,
Their joy is unconfined.

The perfect heralds of Easter joy
Are beautiful on high.
They echo the joy within our hearts
As they ring through the sky.

They sing that Christ has triumphed over
All earthly strife.
How pure and joyous are the bells
Singing eternal life!

Palm Sunday

Kay Hoffman

He wore no royal diadem
Nor kingly robe that day;
Upon a borrowed colt he rode
Along Jerusalem way.

They cast palm branches on his path
And glad hosannas sang;
At last, they thought, their King had come,
An earthly throne to claim.

Yet, there beyond the city gate
Their songs of joy would die
Mid barbs and jeers and crueler taunts,
And shouts of "crucify!"

But on this day he was their king,
This humble, gentle man
Who came to earth to pay sin's price
In God's redemptive plan.

O let us wave palm branches high
And follow in the way;
Jesus of the palm-strewn path
Is passing by today.

PALM SUNDAY

"He Is Risen Indeed!"

Pamela Kennedy

Malchus sat on a stone bench in the courtyard of his daughter's home. The late afternoon sun played across his back, easing the arthritic joints that plagued him now. In the area before him, his grandchildren played with wooden dreidels, spinning the toys and squealing with delight when the game turned to the advantage of one or another.

"Father?"

Malchus turned to answer his daughter's voice.

"I've just come from the marketplace. Peter is in Jerusalem again! He asked after your health, Father, and wants to see you. I've invited him for the evening meal."

Malchus' hand raised instinctively to his right ear, rubbing it unconsciously as he had for years. It was a gesture born of wonder and perpetuated by habit. He nodded now at his daughter. "Yes, yes, it will be good to speak with Peter again and hear how the churches are growing."

The children, distracted by their mother's interruption, clustered around their beloved grandfather. "Saba! Saba!" they clamored. "Is Peter really coming to visit?"

Malchus laughed and nodded, tousling dark curls. An impetuous four-year-old climbed onto his lap.

"Tell us the story again, Saba. Tell us how you first met Peter and how you came to be a follower of the Way."

Malchus stroked his right ear again thoughtfully. These days it was sometimes difficult to recall what he had eaten for the morning meal, but those events of thirty years ago were etched indelibly in his mind, clear and vivid yet.

"Saba?" the anxious four-year-old inquired again.

"Yes, yes. I'll tell you how it happened. I was in the service of the high priest, Caiaphas then, and he had ordered me to accompany a large group of men to witness the capture of a blasphemer and breaker of the sacred laws. The man's name was Jesus—an itinerant rabbi from Nazareth. He was a troublemaker we thought, gathering disciples, teaching heresy in the synagogues, preaching across Judea. Some even claimed he healed the sick and raised the dead. But we did not believe."

"Then what, Saba?" his eight-year-old grandchild interrupted.

Malchus continued. "We came upon Jesus at Gethsemane, east of Jerusalem. The torches many of our company carried lit the still night with a ghostly glare. Those who carried clubs and swords pressed forward, ready to attack if provoked by Jesus' disciples. But Jesus walked toward us calmly, almost as if he expected us. I pressed forward to see more clearly as Judas greeted him with a kiss—a kiss to signal to the arresting officers.

"As the men grabbed Jesus, Peter drew his sword, and as it flashed in the torchlight I felt a searing pain. Blood coursed down the side of my face. I stood still—shocked, stunned."

Malchus' voice faded and again his hand raised to his ear. His eyes held a faraway look, lost in a thirty-year-old drama; his senses still able to hear, feel, and smell that dramatic night.

"And then?" the eight-year-old gently prodded. The children knew the story as well as Malchus, but felt the tension and anxiety afresh each time he told them.

"And then," Malchus continued, "Jesus knelt to the ground and picked up my right ear from the dust. Gently, tenderly as a mother, he placed it beside my bleeding head and as he did so, a searing heat swept through me. 'Be healed, my son,' he said. And his voice was as the wind on a summer night—soft and insistent. Fearfully, I raised my hand to my head and felt there my ear, warm, dry, completely well—as it remains today."

"And Peter? What about Peter, Saba?"

"Jesus spoke to him sternly and said, 'Put your sword back in its place, for all who draw the sword will die by the sword. Do you think I cannot call on my Father, and he will at once put at my disposal more than twelve legions of angels? But how then would the Scriptures be fulfilled that say it must happen in this way?' It was as if a great dark curtain had been lifted from my mind.

All the scriptures I had learned as a child finally made sense. Here was the Promised One, the Messiah. Not only had I seen him, but he touched me, healed not only my body but my soul!"

"And was that when you began to follow in the Way, Saba?" prompted a spellbound child.

"It was when I first believed, my little one. But the following has been a process. After the crucifixion came the resurrection; the undeniable proof of Jesus' claims. And then Peter and the others began to teach what it meant to truly follow Jesus. It takes only a moment to change a mind, my child. Changing your life takes a lifetime. But I have come to understand much because of the final words our Lord spoke to us before he returned to the Father: '. . . surely I will be with you always, to the very end of the age.'"

The children, still transfixed by the drama of their grandfather's story, sat clustered about him, each lost in private thoughts.

It was there, in the garden with the children, that Peter found his one-time adversary and current brother in faith.

"Malchus!" he called, and the startled children scattered like a flock of brown birds.

Malchus raised himself slowly from the bench, his arms outstretched to greet Peter. The two embraced, then parted.

"Shalom, my brother, the Lord is risen!"

"He is risen indeed!" came the warm reply.

Gethsemane

Margaret E. Sangster

The dew lay thick on thorn and flower,
   And where the olives clustered gray
Weird shapes within that awesome hour
   Between the midnight and the day,
Seemed walking phantom-like abroad,
As if to vex the Son of God.

And all the city lay asleep,
   O'er beast and bird the spell was cast,
And nothing stirred the silence deep,
   Save where our Lord the vigil passed;
The long lone vigil when his prayer
Was uttered from a heart's despair.

"Oh, watch with me one little hour!"
   His tender tones had pleading cried
Unto the faithful three whose dower
   Of love had kept them near his side.
Nay—folded hands and drooping head,
And slumber—quiet as the dead.

No wonder then for weariness
   The second time they fall asleep,
He turns in very tenderness,
   And leaves them to repose so deep;
Alone he meets the serpent foe,
Alone he bears the bitter woe.

Gethsemane! Gethsemane!
   We see the glory and the gloom!
Through all thy pain and agony,
   Thy garden wears immortal bloom.
'Twas human friendship failed him there,
But love divine did hear his prayer.

Life's bitter cups we too must take,
   Life's bitter bread in anguish eat;
But when our hearts are like to break
   There comes to us a whisper sweet,
"Fear thou no dim Gethsemane;
Thy sleepless Friend will watch with thee!"

O Zion, that bringest good tidings, get thee up into the high mountain; O Jerusalem, that bringest good tidings, lift up thy voice with strength; lift it up, be not afraid; say unto the cities of Judah, Behold your God!

Isaiah 40:9

Lift up your heads, O ye gates; and be ye lift up, ye everlasting doors; and the King of glory shall come in.

Who is this King of glory? The Lord strong and mighty, the Lord mighty in battle.

Lift up your heads, O ye gates; even lift them up, ye everlasting doors; and the King of glory shall come in.

Who is this King of glory? The Lord of hosts, he is the King of glory. Selah.

Psalm 24:7-10

Comfort ye, comfort ye my people, saith your God.

Speak ye comfortably to Jerusalem, and cry unto her, that her warfare is accomplished, that her iniquity is pardoned: for she hath received of the Lord's hand double for all her sins.

The voice of him that crieth in the wilderness, Prepare ye the way of the Lord, make straight in the desert a highway for our God.

Isaiah 40:1-3

Every valley shall be exalted, and every mountain and hill shall be made low: and the crooked shall be made straight, and the rough places plain:

And the glory of the Lord shall be revealed, and all flesh shall see it together: for the mouth of the Lord hath spoken it.

Isaiah 40:4-5

How Wonderful the Resurrection

Josepha Murray Emms

Suppose there were no Resurrection,
That Christ remained within the tomb,
That human hopes and dreams were fables
Born to fade like ocean spume.

The day would lose its lusty freshness,
The perfumed flowers pale and die,
Gay summer move in frightened zigzags
With clouds across a moody sky.

The world would seem a dreary desert,
Hope flounder in the human heart,
And words would hold no lilting cadence
With love no longer to impart.

But Easter opened wide a doorway,
The Master breathed the morning air;
White lilies now proclaim his victory,
And love and joy are everywhere.

How wonderful the Resurrection!
The promise of another spring,
In spite of life's chaotic struggle,
The soul can know full blossoming.

Pilate saith unto them, What shall I do then with Jesus which is called Christ? They all say unto him, Let him be crucified.

And the governor said, Why, what evil hath he done? But they cried out the more, saying, Let him be crucified.

When Pilate saw that he could prevail nothing, but that rather a tumult was made, he took water, and washed his hands before the multitude, saying, I am innocent of the blood of this just person: see ye to it.

Then answered all the people, and said His blood be on us, and on our children.

Then released he Barabbas unto them: and when he had scourged Jesus, he delivered him to be crucified.

Then the soldiers of the governor took Jesus into the common hall, and gathered unto him the whole band of soldiers.

And they stripped him, and put on him a scarlet robe.

And when they had platted a crown of thorns, they put it upon his head, and a reed in his right hand: and they bowed the knee before him, and mocked him, saying, Hail, King of the Jews!

And they spit upon him, and took the reed, and smote him on the head.

And after that they had mocked him, they took the robe off from him, and put his own raiment on him, and led him away to crucify him.

And as they came out, they found a man of Cyrene, Simon by name: him they compelled to bear his cross.

And when they were come unto a place called Golgotha, that is to say, a place of a skull,

They gave him vinegar to drink mingled with gall: and when he had tasted thereof, he would not drink.

And they crucified him, and parted his garments, casting lots: that it might be fulfilled which was spoken by the prophet, They parted my garments among them, and upon my vestures did they cast lots.

And sitting down they watched him there;

And set up over his head his accusation written, THIS IS JESUS THE KING OF THE JEWS.

Matthew 27:22-37

The Eternal Message

Margaret Rorke

Once again in joy and wonder
    We approach the holy tomb
Where despair's been rent asunder;
    Where a glory lights the gloom;
Where the Marys went at dawning
    On that week's initial day;
Where the sepulcher is yawning
    For its stone's been rolled away.

Once again the angel motions
    To the faithful to draw near
And to offer their devotions
    With the news, "He is not here!"
He has risen! Be not fearful.
    As he promised he has done.
Be not sick at heart or tearful.
    His great victory is won.

Once again we thank our Master
    For the message Easter gives.
Though there's heartbreak and disaster
    For each one of us who lives,
We can glimpse eternal portals
    Through a faith which makes it known
That what means the most to mortals
    Isn't earthbound by a stone.

Come unto me, all ye that labour and are heavy laden, and I will give you rest.

Take my yoke upon you, and learn of me; for I am meek and lowly in heart: and ye shall find rest unto your souls.

Matthew 11:28-29

. . . I am the resurrection, and the life: he that believeth in me, though he were dead, yet shall he live:

And whosoever liveth and believeth in me shall never die . . .

John 11:25-26

And with great power gave the apostles witness of the resurrection of the Lord Jesus: and great grace was upon them all.

Acts 4:33

. . . Worthy is the Lamb that was slain to receive power, and riches, and wisdom, and strength, and honour, and glory, and blessing.

And every creature which is in heaven, and on the earth, and under the earth, and such as are in the sea, and all that are in them, heard I saying, Blessing, and honour, and glory, and power, be unto him that sitteth upon the throne, and unto the Lamb for ever and ever.

Revelation 5:12-13

. . . let us run with patience the race that is set before us,

Looking unto Jesus the author and finisher of our faith; who for the joy that was set before him endured the cross, despising the shame, and is set down at the right hand of the throne of God.

Hebrews 12:1-2

Delights of Easter

Elisabeth Weaver Winstead

Frisky bunnies with ears that flop,
Easter baskets with grass on top;

Wooly lambs with tinkly bells,
Easter song in chorus swells;

Yellow ducks with orange feet
Looking for a tempting treat;

Downy chicks, wiggly and fluffy,
Colored balloons, bouncy and puffy;

Cottontail Peter hopping along
Singing his happy Easter song;

The Easter Bunny stopping to chat
Of Easter eggs and his new hat:

Joyous Easter always brings
A day of such delightful things.

Photo Opposite
CHILDHOOD DELIGHTS
FPG International

The Easter Bunny

Margaret Rorke

Tonight a furry little gent
With big and floppy ears
Will hop his way into the homes
Where childhood still appears.
He's worked all week at dyeing eggs;
His kitchen is a mess.
The sink is full of pots and pans,
And all is stickiness.

By now he's put his ribbon on,
And started on his way
With baskets that he wove by hand
In colors very gay.
Inside each one some candy chicks
And choc'late rabbits sit
On finely shredded paper grass
Where jelly beans permit.

Behind the chairs and davenports
When Easter's sun shall rise,
The little ones will seek and find
Those gifts with joyful cries.
Back home for now another year,
His trip a great success,
The Easter Bunny still must face
That awful kitchen mess.

Bunnytown

Patricia Rose Mongeau

A little girl is filled with joy
On bonny Easter Day
When she arises to many surprises
She finds in bright array:
A basket sweet with things to eat
And eggs of every hue
Made by bunnies in Bunnytown
Who work the whole year through.

From rainbows high up in the sky
They gather colors bright;
And, need I say, 'til Easter Day
They paint from morn to night.
They paint with ease—designed to please
The children Easter Day.
In colors bold they paint things gold,
Brown, yellow, orange, and gray,

And the brightest green you've ever seen,
The gayest red and blue.
When they're done, then on each one
They paint a picture, too.
Then one morn at crack of dawn
They hop along their way
With eggs and sweets and special treats
For children Easter Day!

Fancy Free

Ruth B. Field

Small child with limpid eyes and halo-hair,
What is the subtle magic you possess?
Within your eyes, what secrets are mirrored there?
The simple things so fancifully you dress.

You say there are "flutterbys" on golden wings.
The kitten, you say, leaves his motor running.
On your hand small treasure often strings:
Once a polka-dotted bug a-sunning,

And a snail that had a television set.
You saw a "candle-fly" one night.
A puddle couldn't possibly be wet
For it was full of sky, blue and bright.

A spider did some wonderful crochet—
You saw its doily spread upon the lawn.
The mountain swallowed all the light of day.
And the cat, at night, had his headlights on.

Easter Hat

Esta McElrath

A little girl with freckled nose,
Curly hair, cheeks like a rose,
Wore a hat with upturned brim,
Morning glories and ribbon trim.

She went to church on Easter Day;
Her feet were light, her heart was gay.
She walked along with buoyant tread
As down the aisle the usher led.

A look of joy upon her face,
Within the pew she took her place.
All eyes were turned with knowing smiles
To see a girl so smart in style.

The Egg Hunt

Leona Bernell

The big egg hunt is so much fun—
A part of Easter's joys;
It is a very special time
In the lives of girls and boys.

When all the eggs are colored and
Are hidden out of sight,
The children dash around and 'round
And hunt with all their might.

Under the chair, behind a vase,
Upon a tabletop,
An egg just might be anywhere,
And children cannot stop.

The final count is interesting,
For winners all get toys.
Yes, certainly, the big egg hunt
Is one of Easter's joys.

Funny
Little Rabbits

Naomi E. McElreath

Down by the brook where fern fronds sway,
Little Easter rabbits love to play.
While nibbling at this and nibbling at that,
Choice little bits will make them fat.

Their cunning little noses twitch and wiggle;
You expect every moment that they will giggle.
But hard as you try, no sound do you hear
Save the velvety flipping of a slim little ear.

One ear may be up and one ear down;
It seems they are trying to act like clowns.
I wonder why Easter rabbits act so funny;
Don't you guess it's the way of a bunny?

Spring Kite

Georgia B. Adams

Up, up it goes into the blue
And almost out of sight;
The winds of March are tugging hard
Upon the sturdy kite.

It dances merrily, oh, see
Its whipping, lashing tail.
While winds blow through a small boy's hair . . .
He's laughing with the gale.

I see the wonder fill his eyes;
He's just a lad, you know.
I, too, stood there with my own kite
Not many years ago.

Up, up it goes and out of sight;
I hear his shouts of glee!
A boy, a kite, a happy heart,
And March winds blowing free.

The Flower Show

A.J. Christianson

When the snow has melted
   Under April sun,
And gentle April showers
   Make the clear brooks run,

When the first plump robin
   Chirps his gay hello,
Then the curtain rises
   On the flower show.

Violets and crocuses
   Introduce the theme;
Daffodils and tulips
   Are such a sprightly team.

Purple lilac clusters
   Perfume the springtime air;
Buttercups and daisies
   Are dancing everywhere.

Rambler roses climb up
   On a latticed wall;
Hollyhocks and cosmos
   Stand up straight and tall,

Photo Overleaf
SUPERSTITION MOUNTAINS
ARIZONA
Ed Cooper Photo

Marigolds and sweet peas,
    Zinnias and phlox,
And sunny-hued nasturtiums
    Flaunt in a window box.

And when Autumn breezes
    Bring their first faint chill,
And the crimson sumac
    Flames across the hill,

Gold and bronze chrysanthemums,
    Donning rich array,
Vie with purple asters
    In a royal display.

Then, in scarlet tunics,
    Salvias appear,
In a glowing tribute
    To the waning year.

And, on cue as ever,
    Winter, bowing low,
Drops the final curtain
    On the flower show.

Only Flowers

Gail Robert Yohe

"There is a need," the old man said,
"For spirit-lifting things,
For bits of beauty here and there,
Or scent of perfume in the air,
Or happy voice that sings.

"And this is why," the old man said,
"I work throughout the hours,
Tending garden, row on row,
Digging with my sharp, bright hoe,
Raising naught but flowers.

"Let others do the mundane tasks
That lie within their powers.
Let them produce the food to eat;
I think one's life is not complete
Without a glimpse of flowers."

Photo Opposite
WALKWAY BEAUTY
Gottlieb Hampfler
H. Armstrong Roberts, Inc.

Country Chronicle

Lansing Christman

Spring comes to relax the taut sinews of winter. Loud liquid music replaces the low murmuring chords of water muffled by ice or snow. The hills themselves seem to rejoice at the release.

The March snowmelt transforms our creek into flowing rumbling song when the ice breaks up. Water carries huge ice cargoes swirling with the current down steep cascades. Spring unlocks the chains that held the stream icebound during winter's cold.

The thaw persists. We watch the melt intensify as a warming sun drives its penetrating rays into the snow that blankets the land. The heat penetrates hard, crusted drifts built by winds behind hedges and walls.

Spring is at work above the snow and under, sending the water down slopes into ditches and brooks that feed the stream. There the pressure of the incessant flow builds and foams until the ice heaves and cracks, and then starts to move. The freshet is underway.

Cumbersome cakes of ice thump and bump as they thunder downstream over the waterfalls. They roll and tumble with the surging turbulence. They grind over boulders in the gorge left by the glaciers of an ancient time.

Mists rise from every cascade as the water plunges on toward rivers that feed the sea. The freshness of the spray brings the aroma of soil and stone, of meadow, pasture, and woodland.

The sun is at work. The days are longer. The air is warmer. Creeks and brooks sing crisp and clear as the natural world responds to vernal tenderness. The birds and the land sense it. So do roots and bulbs, and the peepers in swamps and bogs. Humans, too, respond to this renewal of life. Spring is an intensely profound experience.

Easter Breadboard

Butterhorns

- 1 ounce cake yeast
- ¾ cup plus 2 tablespoons sugar
- 2 cups flour
- 1 cup butter, softened
- 2 eggs, separated
- 1 teaspoon vanilla
- ¼ cup chopped nuts
- 1 teaspoon cinnamon

Dissolve yeast in ¼ cup warm water and 2 tablespoons sugar. Add flour, softened butter, and a little salt; mix as pie dough. Add egg yolks, vanilla, and ¼ cup sugar to the yeast mixture; mix well and divide into thirds. Roll each out into a long rectangle and cut each piece into 10 or 12 triangles. Make a filling with the egg whites (stiffly beaten), ½ cup sugar, the chopped nuts, and cinnamon. Spread a teaspoonful on each triangle and roll up, placing each on greased pan, point down. Don't allow to rise. Bake at 350° for 15 to 18 minutes and top with icing.

Icing

Mix 1 cup powdered sugar with 1 teaspoon hot water, ¼ teaspoon vanilla, and ¼ teaspoon almond extract. Drizzle on rolls while they are still warm for a shiny glaze.

Butter Pastry

- ½ cup butter
- 1 cup flour
- 1 egg yolk
- ¼ teaspoon salt
- 1 tablespoon sugar
- ½ teaspoon baking powder
- 2 cups fresh fruit, sliced (apples, peaches, berries)
- Streusel

Combine ingredients (except fruit) and mix as pie dough. Pat into greased 8″ x 8″ pan. Top with fruit and sprinkle with streusel. Bake at 350° for 30 to 40 minutes.

Streusel

With fingers, mix 1 cup sugar, 2 tablespoons flour, 1 teaspoon cinnamon, and 2 tablespoons butter.

Apple Cake

- ½ cup butter
- ¼ cup sugar
- 2 eggs
- ¾ cup flour
- ¾ teaspoon baking powder
- 1 teaspoon vanilla
- 3 to 4 apples, peeled and sliced

Cream butter with the sugar; add eggs. Stir in flour, baking powder, and vanilla; mix well. Spread half of dough in 8″ x 8″ greased pan. Cover with rows of apple slices, top with remainder of dough and spread as well as possible. Dough is soft and will cover apples while baking. Bake at 350° for 30 minutes. Cool, and spread with a thin icing.

Cinnamon Loaf

- 1 ounce cake yeast
- ½ cup shortening
- 1 cup sugar
- 2 teaspoons salt
- 3 egg yolks, well beaten
- 2 cups lukewarm milk
- 7 cups flour
- ½ cup melted butter
- 2 teaspoons cinnamon
- 1 egg yolk

Dissolve yeast in ½ cup lukewarm water. Cream together the shortening and ½ cup sugar. Add to yeast mixture along with salt, egg yolks, and milk. Add flour and beat ingredients well, then knead slightly and allow to rise until double in bulk. Divide dough into six parts and roll each part out into a long rectangle. Brush with the melted butter, then combine the remainder of the sugar with cinnamon and sprinkle some of this on each piece. Fold the outer edges of the dough together to form six long rolls. Place three rolls together and form a braid, pinching the dough together at top and bottom. Repeat with the other three rolls; place on greased cookie sheets or in greased pans. Brush with mixture of one egg yolk and 1 teaspoon water; sprinkle with more sugar and cinnamon. Bake at 350° for 45 minutes.

Photo Opposite
CINNAMON LOAF, BUTTERHORNS, MARY'S FILLED DOUGHNUTS
from *Simply Delicious Cookbook*, copyright © 1976 by Ideals Publishing Corp., Nashville, Tennessee

My God Walked through the Garden

Georgia B. Adams

Just as the nighttime shadows
Were gently giving way
To early morning sunrise
At breaking of the day,

My God walked through the garden,
Through grasses green and cool;
And everywhere I wandered,
His gentle touch was seen.

He swept the earth with dewdrops;
He woke the sleeping flowers.
One word brought forth the sunshine
To brighten morning hours.

He nodded to the birdlife
And they began to sing;
The garden came alive with
The breath of early spring.

Gone are the nighttime shadows,
The gloom was cast away,
As God walked through the garden
At breaking of the day.

Cherry Trees

Stella Craft Tremble

The trees are busy all year long
With leaves and fruit and flowers;
They entertain the birds and bees
Through fragrant sunny hours.

Unselfish are they—pleased to give
For nests, a hidden space,
In summertime beneath their arms,
A cool and shady place.

They bow and visit with the winds,
Laugh softly with the breeze,
Then hold the sunlight as it shines
Upon the trembling leaves.

In spring, they throw a little shower
Of snowy blossoms white,
Caught by the tender grass below
Which holds them with delight.

Photo Opposite
TREES IN BLOOM
Gene Ahrens

Spring Fever

Edgar A. Guest

Once in a while I think it is good for a man's soul to play hooky. Maybe the Lord knew that and fixed this earth so there would occasionally be attractions on it no man of us could resist. Some like to go fishing. Some like to play golf. Some are for the baseball game, but no man has ever been born so poor on this earth that life did not have some joy to give him.

But how strange it all is, while every one of us looks forward to pleasure as the ultimate end of striving, it is only occasionally that he can enjoy it. If he were bound to pleasure as he is bound to work, he would grow to hate it. Golf is only good to play when man can leave his work behind. A man who has nothing to do but to play golf in time deserts the game. It has become boredom to him. So would fishing, for the fisherman who has to do it for a living it is work. The only thrill in the catch is the profit it will bring.

So, on a warm spring day, when the skies are blue and the breeze sweet with the first faint hint of fragrance, the boy in me insists on making holiday. Neither duty nor profit can hold me longer. Even at the risk of failure I yearn to cut loose from obligation and necessity, and take such a day selfishly to myself.

When the blue gets back in the skies once more
And the vines grow green 'round the kitchen door,
When the roses bud and the robins come,
I stretch myself and I say: "Ho-hum!
I ought to work but I guess I won't;
Though some want riches today, I don't;
This looks to me like the sort of day
That was made to idle and dream away."

When the sun is high and the air just right,
With the trees all blossomy, pink and white,
And the grass, as soft as a feather bed
With the white clouds drifting just overhead,
I stretch and yawn like a school boy then,
And turn away from the walks of men
And tell myself in a shamefaced way:
"I'm going to play hooky from work today!

"Here is a morning too rare to miss,
And what is gold to a day like this,
And what is fame to the things I'll see
Through the latticework of a fine old tree?
There is work to do, but the work can wait;
There are goals to reach, there are foes to hate,
There are hurtful things which the smart might say,
But nothing like that shall spoil today.

"Today I'll turn from the noisy town
And just put all of my burdens down;
I'll quit the world and its common sense,
And the things men think are of consequence,
To chum with birds and the friendly trees
And try to fathom their mysteries,
For here is a day which looks to be
The kind I can fritter away on me."

Floating Flower

Mina Morris Scott

A butterfly is like a floating flower,
A blossom freed in some enchanted hour
From off the vernal stem and flung to space,
A brilliant thing of airy, winsome grace.

Though on the summer breezes it may roam,
It feels itself most naturally at home
When it can snuggle in a flower's heart—
The two can then be scarcely told apart.

The bright translucence of the quivering wing
Can match in splendor every petaling
On which it comes to rest
As lightly as a leaf is breeze-caressed.

Nature's Church

Florence H. Steelman

I went to church in the woods today;
I didn't hear a preacher pray,
Nor a sermon from the blessed Book,
But I heard the murmur of a brook.

I walked among a host of trees
Which formed a canopy of leaves
Above my head, and in that place
A feeling came of joy and grace.

The choir I heard was the song of birds —
The sweetest notes, no need of words.
Their feathered throats trilled high with
  praise,
Till my voice, too, I had to raise.

And then I knelt in the mossy sod
In that cathedral built by God.
The light of peace in me was born
Among the woods this Sabbath morn.

The Sun upon the Road

Byrne K. Brooke

I watched it as it stole along
Into a clump of trees,
Where it magnified the glory
Of a nest of bumblebees.

Then smilingly it glided
To where the river ran,
And there upon the waters
It spread a golden fan.

A ray of light it left behind
To warm a sleepy toad,
And when I looked again I saw
The sun upon the road.

It turned the dust into a mass
Of finely-sprinkled gold;
The magic of that wondrous scene
No one could e'er enfold.

So when the world looks dreary
And heavy seems my load,
I gaze afar until I see
The sun upon the road!

Memories of Mother

As the years go by, we carry the memories of our mothers close to our hearts. But do we ever add up all the little things they've done for us? Like patching scraped knees and broken hearts, driving little ones to birthday parties and music lessons, teaching the skills and pleasures of gardening, teaching us about God and values. And all of this is offered with love.

In our next issue, *Mother's Day Ideals*, we honor and celebrate all mothers. How appropriate that a day in May, in the fullness of springtime, is set aside for Mother's Day. We hope you will join us as we share this special occasion with readers like Mrs. Pearl C. Breland, of Ridgeland, South Carolina, who writes

> I *thoroughly enjoy* Ideals *magazine. It is next in line to my bible . . . truly soothing to my soul.*

And Mr. Harold Lorenz, of Jackson, Missouri, who writes

> Ideals *magazine is . . . uplifting, understandable . . . cheerful, exciting, and I always look forward to the next issue.*

Thank you Mrs. Breland and Mr. Lorenz. Sharing Ideals with you is an honor. We hope our other readers will help us share I*deals* with their friends by starting a gift subscription with *Mother's Day.*

ACKNOWLEDGMENTS

MY GOD WALKED THROUGH THE GARDEN from *THE SILVER FLUTE AND OTHER POEMS* by Georgia B. Adams, copyright © 1968. Used by permission; RESTLESS from *CHALLENGE OF THE SEASONS* by Dorothy Bettencourt Elfstrom, copyright © 1963. Used by permission; SPRING FEVER from *EDGAR A. GUEST BROADCASTING,* copyright 1935, The Reilly & Lee Co. Used by permission; EASTER DAY PRAYER from *THE PRAYERS OF PETER MARSHALL,* edited and with prefaces by Catherine Marshall, copyright © 1954, 1982 by Catherine Marshall LeSourd. Published by Chosen Books, Fleming H. Revell Company. Used by permission; THE ETERNAL MESSAGE from *AN OLD CRACKED CUP* by Margaret Rorke, copyright © 1980 by Northwood Institute Press. Used by permission; GETHSEMANE from *EASTER BELLS* by Margaret E. Sangster, copyright 1897 by Harper & Brothers, New York; Stella Craft Tremble for CHERRY TREES from *THORNS AND THISTLEDOWN,* copyright 1954. Used by permission; MIGRANT BEAUTY from *UNFORGETTABLE ECHOES* copyright by Cora Ellen Wells. Used by permission. Our sincere thanks to the following whose addresses we were unable to locate: Leona Bernell for THE EASTER EGG HUNT; Byrne K. Brooke for THE SUN UPON THE ROAD; A.J. Christianson for THE FLOWER SHOW; RENDEZVOUS from *FINDING BEAUTY* by Grace E. Easley, copyright © 1974; Catherine Grayman for APRIL RECIPE; Carol Ann Kimball for ONE; Esta McElrath for EASTER HAT; Naomi E. McElreath for FUNNY LITTLE RABBITS; Patricia Rose Mongeau for EASTER; Leone Monroe for SMALL GREEN THUMB; Florence H. Steelman for NATURE'S CHURCH from *DRIFTWOOD;* Gail Robert Yohe for ONLY FLOWERS.